In You, GOD's Trust

Book 2

Michelline Jacquelle
"Michelle" Porter

Copyright © 2017. All rights reserved.

No part of this publication may be reproduced, stored in a retrieval system or transmitted in any way by any means, electronic, mechanical, photocopy, recording or otherwise, without the prior permission of the author except as provided by USA copyright law.

The opinions expressed by the author are not necessarily those of Revival Waves of Glory Books & Publishing.

Published by Revival Waves of Glory Books & Publishing

PO Box 596 | Litchfield, Illinois 62056 USA

www.revivalwavesofgloryministries.com

Revival Waves of Glory Books & Publishing is committed to excellence in the publishing industry.

Book design Copyright © 2017 by Revival Waves of Glory Books & Publishing. All rights reserved.

Published in the United States of America

Paperback: 978-1546792741

"And as the surface of an object
provides clear vision,
so shall I."

— Michelline J. Porter

Table of Contents

I. THE PRINCIPAL 7

II. ORDINATION 11

III. COMMUNION 17

IV. BENEDICTION 21

In You, GOD's Trust: Book 2

Composition of Trials

The Principal
Ordination
Communion
Benediction

I.
THE PRINCIPAL

Fundamental evaluation is allocated with a basic value - a predetermined capital - a _Principal_ (primary budget into expenditure). Life arrives with credit - a _Trust_. This grant then allows treasures to be disbursed into forthright investments.

I am thankful.

I am appreciative of my environment and circumstances.

I am anxious to learn – and willing to grow.

Gifted with natural value,

I recognize my self.

And through self-evaluation, I am acquainted with the factors that I am composed of.

I inherit what is inherent.

I am primed with intelligence and vitality; my most valuable resources.

I am to accomplish proficiency with the usage of my tools.

I gather my conscious and prepare for future endeavors.

I understand that I must accept proper timing
of growth and achievement.

My trials are unique.

To encounter challenge is to endure test of faith within myself and my aspiration to persevere.

And so, I am thankful.

II.
ORDINATION

With principal intact, the arrangement and administration of essentials rely upon ***Ordination***.

Distinctive adjustments are gained.

Value is observed in a number of ventures. Preparations are made to produce and protect investments.

I am stimulated to begin a march of conformity.

For induction stimulates currency.

And so I walk in the deepest of night.

I know to escape what preys upon me.

And for miles, I walk -

And with child in my belly,

I seek shelter.

For any moment, she is to be birthed.

And in the heat of day, I walk -

And for miles

And with her in my belly,

I seek resources.

For forty weeks of seven days of twelve and twelve hours is a trial within itself.

An obligation in this duration.

For to be ordained, I bear the weight of my own.

I am capable through self-motivation.

For I think beyond my burdens.

I know that strength is amplified through application of pressure.

I must gather mentality.

I endure fitness.

Guided by intuition,

I am aware of the natural discipline of nature.

And so, I gather perception of those who embody testosterone.

For multiple heads are indeed better than one.

And I am lifted.

A border is now crossed.

And on this land, I say "Shalom".

Within this altered mindset,
accountability is a prerequisite.

I choose to leave behind insolent behavior that may lie within -

So as to avoid the ripple of disastrous events.

For if pride destroys man, then pride shall be swallowed.

For stigma shall be no longer.

It shall be devoured with humble acceptance.

I accept challenges.

And I challenge my capabilities through self-motivation.

For I am confident in my skills.

I come to know the potential of my strength.

And so, I know what is to be fulfilled.

I am to conduct exchange in order to ensure my safety and protection.

III.
COMMUNION

Exchange of information is invaluable.

In *Communion*, there is advisory as well as encouragement. With fruitful interaction, productive structure is then earned. Greater shares are sustained through union.

I encounter a collection of individuals.

Within this sum, we shall communicate.

For in community, I am to engage.

And I must not ignore the concept of social beings:

Exchange and Productivity;

Togetherness and Support.

I offer compliance.

For camaraderie is social appreciation.

And we shall receive nourishment together.

I am driven to contribute what is reasonable and within my means.

I present myself with precision

I am impelled to bring to the table what others   may benefit from.

And amiable transaction must take place.

Trade occurs foreign and local.

And so I endure healthy competition,

Objectives provide motivation.

It is rational to plan ahead.

My hands shall remain ample as I accrue
and replenish resources.

I share within my capacity –
Supplying and retrieving wise investments.

I understand the convenience of services
rendered.

Continuance of amiable transaction shall
indeed promote credibility.

An affluent society is one with a healthy
flow of exchange of goods.

And bond and surety is likely through
appreciation of value of others.

IV.
BENEDICTION

Tokens of admiration provide endorsement of good deeds. _Benediction_ provides devotion for praise and approval.

There is profit in prosperity.

There is sanctity in support.

I have stored necessary provisions.

As my proportions are sufficient,
I propose altruistic notion.

In benevolence, I see giving.

I grasp, without choice, that I must accept
what I cannot modify.

My heart dwells in empathy.

And I know to provide support for those who are unable. For I am an advocate. Social assistance shall be welcomed.

In selfless nature, there is expected donation.

I exercise initiative to contribute to efficiency of ecosystem.

A non-requirement to live;

A moral requirement for appreciation and salvation.

I acknowledge what I hold in my hand.

To know copper is to know the elemental characteristics and energy capacity.

I hold ability to invent.

And what is not defined as broken,
I can enhance!

With vast resources, I shall open doors for those who utilize skills.

A means of establishment may be introduced –

As a realm of assignments is gainful for all participants.

A well planned structure shall prove to be rewarding.

Within systems I create, I shall require accountability, safety, proper training and preparation.

I build clear, concise instructions.

I am mature in my expectations within individuality.

I support achievement.

Sincerity remains in my dealings.

I praise my Creator.

For my Creator gives unto me,
so that I am able to disburse.

May peace be with you in all that you do.

Be wise to know what you contain within your independent structure.

Prepare your mentality and physicality for burdens of life.

Appreciate your surroundings, and understand

your importance within your environment.

Give within your means, and acknowledge the lands that have sustained your life as well as the lives that surround you.

www.ingramcontent.com/pod-product-compliance
Lightning Source LLC
LaVergne TN
LVHW021749060526
838200LV00052B/3553